# ED GEIN

The True Crime Story of

the Gruesome Serial Killer and Body Snatcher

## HUNTER HANSON

# Table of Contents

# Introduction

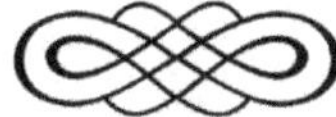

The human heart is capable of greatness and compassion and love. But the human heart is also capable of some truly horrible things.

If you're like most people, you live your life simply assuming that your friends and family and neighbors are average people. Sure, they have bad days and they make faulty decisions and they sometimes do things they regret. No one is perfect. But when you lay your head down at night, you assume with nearly 100% certainty that people around you are good, hard-working, whole-hearted people.

They're not monsters. Because monsters don't exist, right? Monsters are simply the creation of Hollywood and fairy tales and older siblings trying to get a rise out of you around a campfire at night.

However, there is an ugly and undeniable truth about the world that festers right below its surface: monsters do exist, they are around us, and they can harm us. Not only are they capable of truly tremendously vicious and horrible things, they can strike without any reason or warning. They can end lives in a heartbeat in the most inhumane and shocking ways.

And these monsters which can snuff any of us out without a care in the world aren't hidden in the sewers or lurking in a dark, decrypted house or haunted forest. No, the monsters that can do the most harm to us and our loved ones live all around us. In houses and apartments, driving cars and attending jobs. You see them at the grocery store but you don't know it. You pass them at a streetlight but you have no idea. You might even wave to them and tell them hello, unaware that you have just crossed paths with a person who carries a heavy darkness inside them, aching to infect others and inflict their pain upon them.

Everyone is aware that serial killers exist. We all have told and heard the tales from youth about someone who snapped, went crazy, slaughtered dozens and then was apprehended by the authorities and locked away, a boogey man hidden in confinement never to see the light of day again.

When we think of these people, these monsters, we usually picture a wild-eyed, crazed individual. Someone who laughs maniacally when others are hurt or shows not a single ounce of remorse at the pain they've caused. But that's only a half-truth, that doesn't tell the whole picture of who these people are.

When you get down to it, some of the people who have done the worst things in human history look just like me and you. They come across as normal and completely run of the mill. Maybe they're a bit more quiet or maybe they keep to themselves. Perhaps they come across as shy, reserved, lacking the urge to be the center of attention.

How strange, then, that a vast tempest of fury and rage builds inside them. A massive hurricane of an insatiable desire to hurt others. Even with such a placid and calm demeanor, a ravenous creature stirs beneath.

If you want to sum up Ed Gein, that would be the best way to do it. He was a quiet man, a calm man, someone who you wouldn't look twice at while waiting at a bus stop beside him. He didn't impose, he didn't intimate, he didn't threaten and he hardly ever raised his voice, let alone his fist.

Well, in public that is.

Ed Gein is a perfect example of the great dichotomy of the human condition. How can someone seem so normal, so perfectly sane, while still doing such horrendous crimes? How can someone like Gein be created so evil from birth? Because surely someone like that isn't transformed into the monster he was, right? What sort of circumstances would do that to a human? What sort of tragic tale would need to be told to warp someone's heart and soul?

The truth is that Gein's story is both completely unremarkable while also hard to believe. In many ways, when you really look back at his life, the idea that he would become such a beast hidden under the mask of formality isn't that shocking at all. When you look at how he was raised, what he endured, and the sort of predisposition he had, the end results of Gein are not that surprising at all.

The facts are this: Ed Gein is responsible for at least two murders and suspected of at least seven more. That is a shocking number of deaths at his hands.

But it's not just the number that he killed that has etched him into the annals of America's darkest history. It's the way he did it. It's *why* he did it. Sadly, Gein's body count pales in comparison to some of the other serial killers you have likely heard of. But while he never inflicted damage to as many poor souls as the Son of Sam or the Night Stalker or the BTK Killer, he performed his wicked deeds in such cruel and terrifying ways that his name lives on to this day as a figure of pure nightmare.

Gein has inspired—if you can use that word—Hollywood and pop culture in ways that few other infamous figures in our history have. He has transformed the idea of what a serial killer can be and how they can act. He has grabbed hold of the public's consciousness like a monster under a bed grabs onto the ankles of an unsuspecting child.

For many reasons, our culture just cannot shake Ed Gein or his story. Why? What is it about him? What is it that keeps us coming back to him again and again? Why does this quiet, meek murderer still get talked about today?

To understand that you need to understand Gein and what made him the man he was and how he did the atrocious acts we still recall in horror to this day. That means you need to be brave, hold on tight, and learn about the life of Ed Gein. It won't always be easy and it won't ever be pretty, but it will shed light on the man who became a terrifying legend.

Before he was the Butcher of Plainfield or the Plainfield Ghoul, he was just regular old Edward Theodore Gein. A man who was either built differently or scarred tremendously. A man that became more monster than human and left a terror in his wake.

PART ONE

# The Discovery

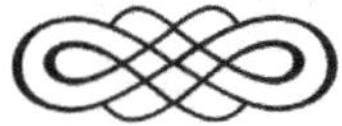

Winters in Wisconsin can get cold. Even if you have never visited the Badger State, you are surely aware of that. From the snow to the wind and the persistence of each, Wisconsin will not go easy on you. And the vast farmlands that dot the entire state are some of the coldest places in the region. It is no shock when parts of the state reach zero degrees long before the new year and Christmastime.

Despite that, the residents of this state just go about their lives and their work, bundling up and pushing through the cold and living a normal life.

But there was nothing normal about one cold November day back in the 1950s. It was downright chilling—but for reasons other than the temperature.

Weeks had been leading up to this moment. The detectives and officers on the scene were beyond nervous; they were shaking. Some people thought the law enforcement officials were shivering and that's why they seemed to be withdrawn, quiet, and on edge. That might have been part of it. But that wasn't all of it.

No, the officers were acting so cold because there was a bitter terror chilling their hearts as their automobiles rolled down the long, frozen dirt road in Plainfield, Wisconsin. The brave cops and detectives showed up at Ed Gein's run-down farm on a blistering cold November 17, 1957. They weren't coming there to have a chat or receive evidence or anything cordial. In their heart of hearts, many of them knew they were about to go face to face with a ruthless killer. And a long path that had many false starts and stops and many shattered hearts and lives could be finally reaching its conclusion.

# The Kidnapping

The cars slowed as the cops arrived and got closer to the front door. In those final moments before climbing out of their automobiles, they got their thoughts together and remembered why they were there. It was serious. Deadly serious, in fact. Gein was a suspect in the theft of a nearby hardware shop and, more importantly, the absence of the owner, Bernice Worden. Worden had been missing and the family was terribly worried. As for Gein, he had become the suspect over time, mostly because he had been the hardware store's final client and had been observed hanging about the area.

Kidnappings are very serious business for law enforcement. It's a tough situation because it is never known—until the very end—if the person is just simply missing or deceased. That means that finding a missing person needs to be handled quickly, it's truly a matter of life or death. The county's sheriff, Arthur Schley, was certainly handling the case with care. Like many others in Plainfield, Schley actually knew Worden personally. She was a good woman with many friends, many family members and was the type of person who would never harm a fly. She was also 50 years old and not one to just suddenly vanish for no reason at all.

All signs pointed to Gein being a part of the disappearance. The investigation had started when Bernice's son entered the hardware shop at 5:00 p.m. on November 16th. He had gotten reports that the shop's store truck had been driven away early that morning and that no one had been in or out since then.

When Bernice's son, Deputy Sheriff Frank Worden, entered the store, he saw something alarming and downright terrifying. Something that no child ever wants to find when they are looking for their parents: the cash register was wide open and there were blood stains below it on the ground.

The authorities were called and Sheriff Schley arrived. That is when the investigation began. Soon, there were clues pointed directly at local resident Ed Gein, the quiet man that kept to himself out on the farmhouse a few miles outside of town.

Gein had been in the store the evening before and was set to come back and return a gallon of antifreeze the next morning. That was clue number one that he was somehow there and involved with Bernice's disappearance the next day. But the evidence that was even more damning was from the morning after, when Bernice disappeared. A sales slip for a gallon of antifreeze happened to be the last receipt written by Bernice. It was about as much of a smoking gun as authorities could hope to find and it proved that Ed Gein was most certainly the last person to see Mrs. Bernice alive.

The cops around town raced to find Gein. As mentioned, they knew that the sooner they found him, the better the chances of them finding Bernice, dead or alive. It was frigid and cold in Wisconsin, no place for a poor, harmed woman to be left alone. They didn't know what had happened to Bernice but they were going to find out—and they were going to have Ed Gein tell them.

Later that day, Gein was shopping at a local store. The quiet man was wearing a warm wool hat, a jacket, and was quietly wandering down the aisle buying his groceries when a stream of cops came in and found him. They told him to place his hands behind his back and whisked him out of the store.

It remains to be known if Gein was aware of what had been discovered. Surely there must have been something in his mind that told him he had finally been caught and his years of harming others had come to an end. But if he was panicked or scared, he certainly didn't show it. Like all things Gein did, he remained reticent and withdrawn as he was placed in the back of a squad car.

Meanwhile, across town the cops began their race out to Gein's farmhouse, not sure of what they would find but prepared for anything.

## Entering the House of Horrors

When Sheriff Schley and his crew approached the front steps of the house, they immediately felt like something was wrong. From the outside, the farmhouse didn't look too out of shape or bizarre. But there was an odd feeling that permeated from inside, like a twisted fireplace that was eternally lit by some sort of blood red flame.

Something didn't feel right about the Gein house. But no one that had arrived on that day was quite familiar with the farmhouse or the Gein family. They didn't know what the man was capable of. But after years of being alone and being avoided and overlooked, the local cops of Plainfield started to suspect that perhaps this place had been dark and haunted for multiple reasons for many years. They felt like they were about to cross a threshold into something inhumane, shocking, and life-changing.

They were right.

The door slowly opened. The police entered.

Imagine the sound of the cold Wisconsin air, so crisp and brisk that it sounded heavy as it moved through the doorway onto the hardwood floors. Imagine the thump of the heavy door as it tapped against the wall. Thump, thump, thump. Imagine the sound of the boots as they move forward.

The house was quiet, dark. The only illumination was that of the dull grey sky attempting to sneak in, as if it was desperate to bring even the smallest amount of warmth and light into the building. But it did little good, most corners of the farmhouse were black as pitch.

Gein's abandoned farmhouse was a disorganized case study. In other words, it was a complete mess. It looked and felt like a place that hadn't been cleaned in ages, as if the owners had perished and fled long ago. It was hard to believe that someone was actually living in the farmhouse. But what sort of person would be able to exist in such a disaster of a building? Who could live among all the mess and clutter and chaos that existed in every nook and cranny of the farmhouse?

The law enforcement officials were about to find out just what sort of person could live like that. And they weren't going to like the answer they found.

The interior's floor and countertops were covered in trash and decaying waste. Papers stacked high: old newspaper, books, various leaflets, fliers and more. It didn't appear as if Gein ate a whole lot and made a lot of trash but he certainly hadn't had his disposed in some time because random waste and rubbage was everywhere you would look. It was as if someone had come into the house with the sole purpose of making it appear unlivable and abandoned.

Again, the officers on the scene found themselves questioning how anyone could peacefully exist in a place like this.

It was extremely hard to navigate the rooms on foot. The overwhelming stench of squalor and decay was overpowering and several officers had to raise their hands to their noses and mouths to keep the smell out. No one was quite sure what they were looking for. There wasn't the sound of anything stirring, except for maybe an occasional mouse or the scurry of a cockroach across the floorboards. The only other sound was that of the wind trying to find its way into the house, casting a cold on everything it touched.

# Discovering Darkness

Just a few moments into the investigation of the farmhouse, a discovery was made. A grim discovery that would change everything. While cautiously and slowly walking through the house, Sheriff Schley felt something rub against his jacket as he used his flashlight to investigate the cluttered and dilapidated kitchen.

He wasn't sure what it was but he felt a sense of serious unease right away. He knew why he was there, he knew what he could possibly find in a house such as this. Sheriff Schley had never laid eyes upon what he was about to see. And his career had never been close to anything as heinous as the crime about to be uncovered. With slow, measured movements, the sheriff raised his head to see what he had run into. What he saw caught the breath in his throat. Terror gripped him and even this man, a seasoned law enforcement official, was hardly able to make a sound or move. What laid before him was a sizable cadaver that was swinging from the beams upside down. The mutilated body had been gutted, slit open savagely, and the head had been removed.

At first, Schley wasn't sure what he was looking at. Was it a deer's carcass? Was this just the result of a hunting trip out? Those sorts of activities were very common, especially in that part of Wisconsin. But in seconds, reality sank in. It hit the sheriff like a ton of bricks and nearly made his knees buckle. It is rare for anyone, even someone who was so familiar with crime and violence, to see something so disturbing and haunting.

Frank Worden's mother Bernice Worden had been located.

That alone would be enough to throw Gein behind bars for the rest of his life. But in just a short while longer, the cops on the scene discovered that there was so much more lurking in every corner of the house. After discovering Worden's body, the startled deputies came across other horrific findings that made even the most seasoned professional's stomach turn. This was not a house, it was a graveyard. It was a nightmare. It was the most terrifying thing that any of these men had ever seen. There were so many disturbing visions, as if pulled out of someone's worst dreams, everywhere they looked.

The odd-looking bowl in the living room was really the top of a human skull. The trash can and light shades were fashioned out of human skin, prying from the bones of a murder victim and then slung out to dry before being manipulated and turned into decorations. There was more. Indeed, it seemed like Gein's house of horrors wouldn't stop providing new nightmare fuel. A chair made of human skin, preserved female genitalia in a shoebox, a belt crafted from nipples, a severed head, multiple sliced noses, and a heart. It was all kept in pristine condition, as if someone took such precious care with each and every piece of humanity that they stripped from someone else.

## The Crypt

The more they searched the house, the more horrifying awards they discovered. Perhaps nothing was more disturbing than the all-human skin suit that had been created. As they attempted to count the number of women who could have perished at Ed's hands, their minds began to spin.

They had found the poor woman they had been looking for. But they had also found so much more. In just a few moments, these police officers had uncovered one of the most infamous scenes in all of American history. It was something that would be spoken about for years, written about for decades, and would change the way people thought of their soft-spoken neighbors forever.

In the hours following such a nightmarish scene, authorities learned all about the dark, twisted mind of Ed Gein and all he had done during his life. There was no sense in holding back at that point so Gein let it all out. He let a vile darkness pour forth from him, years and years of terrifying work that he had done in secret as Wisconsin and the entire nation was none the wiser. He admitted that between the years 1947 and 1952, he had visited three local cemeteries as many as 40 times. And what did he do there? Well, you can imagine. Gein would trip to the graveyards so he could dig up and exhume recently buried bodies. These were the corpses that would be sliced up, manipulated, and turned into the disgusting decorations that hung throughout his house.

Gein claimed that he was in a "daze-like" state during those late-night visits to the cemetery.

In many ways, this day was the end of Ed Gein. He was obviously someone greatly disturbed, beyond measurable ways. And his reign of terror had come to an end in the most horrific way. But obviously, it didn't start with Bernice Worden. The road to his capture and the trauma that came with it started years before and slowly evolved from a disturbed young man into a homicidal maniac.

PART TWO

# Makings of a Killer

There are many questions that people have asked about Ed Gein throughout the years. Many people have assumed that there could be some clues as to why he ended up the way he did. When the police officers found Bernice Worden and the slaughtered bodies in his home, they were all left speechless and clueless about what sort of things must have happened to create such a monster.

But it was only when more of Gein's dark past came to light that that list of questions grew even more. What had led him to that point living alone in a house full of the dead, cut off from the rest of the world and happy to be surrounded by such haunting images? How did he get to that point? What has altered and shaped his mind in such an awful way to present a human being that desired such dark and twisted things?

Surely, there must be clues to his final outcome in the life that Gein lived. The way he was raised, the way the world treated him, the methods by which he came of age—all of it must have been a contributing factor, right?

It is true that looking back on Gein's life is like a study of someone continually led down a path that is too awful for most people to bear. There were many things that happened to him that would warp him and slowly turn him closer and closer and nearer and nearer to a dark side he couldn't resist. Sure enough, the life that Gein lived for so many years certainly had a direct influence on the creation he would become. Now that so much time has passed, we can look back on his biography and see a series of bumps in the road there leading him to a certain point.

It is important to remember that this sort of examination of Gein just wasn't likely when he was first caught. Why? It was a different time and those in charge of figuring out crimes and why they happen had no interest in anything that could be considered humanizing the suspect. They didn't really want to know *why* the people did the things they did. They were written off as "sick" and that was that. Toss them in jail and throw the key, they would say. Why waste your time on these people, usually called "freaks" and "sickos."

To be clear, there is no excusing the heinous things that Gein did. No matter how troubled his life was or the situation he lived through or the inner turmoil he suffered, nothing gave him the right to do what he did. But to not fully dive into his past, his upbringing, and some serious issues that plagued him from a young age is to not tell the full story. If you want to really know about Ed Gein and what he did, you have to *really know* about him. Is it humanizing to look at his past and figure out how it shaped him? In a way, yes. Then again, he was a human. A truly troubled, terrifying, unhinged human.

So, it is worth asking again and clearly: how can a young person become an Ed Gein? Numerous hints may be gleaned from a detailed examination of his early years and household. To really dig into them all, you have to start at the very beginning.

Augusta and George Gein welcomed Edward Theodore into the world on August 27, 1906 in La Crosse, Wisconsin. He wasn't the first child. The couple had two boys, with Ed being the second. Henry, who was seven years older than Ed, was the first child. In many ways, the life of Ed was like many other young Wisconsin boys at the time. He would participate in school, play in the snow during the winter, go hunting during the warmer season, and typically do the things that other kids do.

He spent a lot of time with his brother too and, years later, people would comment on how they seemed like many other brothers in the area at the time. All American, normal, not really unique in many ways. At least that is how they appeared. The truth is that below the surface and past what the neighbors could see, both Ed and his brother Henry were living a life that was anything but normal. It was anything but serene. It was not the sort of home life that any young boy should be living.

You may have heard in the past that Ed Gein's life and his despicable crimes were the result of his mother. Of course, no one is to blame for the things that Gein did aside from himself. It was his mind that created the dark thoughts that drove him, his feet that walked him to the crime scenes, and his hands that did the murders. But it is hard to look back on his mother and how she treated him and feel like it had nothing to do with the way Gein developed and the man he became.

The truth is that an entire book could be written about Augusta Gein herself. In fact, a book could dive into who she was and why she was the way she was. In fact, the entire family line of the Geins had problems but they were the most apparent in Augusta, who lived a life that was stressful, anxious, and commanded by a strict religious order. She was deeply, deeply religious, and the fervently pious Augusta was also committed to raising her young boys in accordance with her high moral standards. Her entire life lived around religion. But it wasn't just about the glory of Heaven and how great your life could be if you followed God's rules. No, instead she was supremely focused on how bad your life would be if you deviated from God's path.

Augusta saw a world full of sinners. All around her, even in the quiet town she grew up in, people were straying further and further from God's light. She was raised in a very religious way, with a lot of fire and brimstone. It was a deeply unsettling way to grow up and it made her paranoid about all those around her and even herself. She was incredibly hard on others but she was also hard on herself and felt that she was often not doing as God had wanted. She looked on at the world as sinful, cruel, monstrous in many ways. And yet, she still brought children into that world. But upon their births, she became even more fervent in her views and disdain for the corruption she saw all around her.

According to her, Augusta lived in a warped, sickened society where sinners abounded. She lived in constant fear of this dreaded world and knew it posed such a risk not only to her but to her young sons as well. And due to that, she constantly reinforced biblical principles in her boys. When the boys were outside of her watch and with other children who lived nearby, they might play around and seemingly have fun. But behind the closed, heavy door of the Gein house, that wasn't the case at all. There were no games to be played, no joy to spread, no jokes to laugh at or songs to sing. Both Ed and Henry would spend hours reading the Bible, studying the word of God, reciting it back to their mom and then being forcefully punished when they did anything out of line.

She wasn't going to raise sinners, she told them both. The world was a cold and terrible place full of people looking to hurt you and persuade you to go down a path that takes you straight to damnation, she told them. Studying your gospel and going to church could only get you so far, she instilled in the boys. The only thing that could truly prevent the wrath of the sinful world and the pain it could cause was her and her alone. They needed their mother, that was the bottom line. True, she would have to protect them from sin and the work of the devil, but somehow this little woman would be able to do it all single-handedly.

Augusta was teaching her boys that if they strayed from her, they strayed from God. If they ever left her eye, they would soon face a life full of sin and the eternal punishment handed down by God. She was the only one who could truly protect them, she was the only one who could keep them safe. At the same time, she made their lives miserable. She was incredibly strict, as you'd imagine, but the distorted worldview that she had come to see as normal was poisoning the minds of her young boys. She was enforcing such intense rules upon them that they only saw life as a daily challenge of avoiding sin. Augusta continually forbade her kids from having sexual impulses out of concern that they would be sent to hell, warning them about the immorality and looseness of women. This was an approach to parenting that would have severe ramifications on both children, but especially Ed.

He was coming of age to think that everything about adulthood was wrong. He couldn't trust the people he was around because they were sinners. He couldn't trust the normal desires of his own body because they were a pathway to Hell. The pre-teen years are difficult for anyone but they were far harder for Ed because of the challenges that Augusta has presented. Imagine being a young child, having a hard enough time getting through puberty on your own. Imagine how much worse it would be if your mother was constantly telling you that the very normal urges you were feeling were sinful and the world surrounding you was one full of demons in disguise.

You can imagine just how much this would play with a young boy's mind as he attempts to become a man.

As you can tell, Augusta was a harsh, bossy lady who thought her worldview was infallible and accurate. Day in and day out, the Gein house was filled with nothing but intense, scary preaching from Augusta's pulpit. It was her way or the highway. And no one could protest against Augusta because it was, in essence, protesting against God himself. She was fighting on behalf of the Lord, she told everyone. She knew she was right at all times and she had no problem enforcing her convictions on her two children and her husband. At the end of the day, she said that she did all of these things out of love for her boys. But maybe not out of love for her husband. Because her husband was someone she had very limited affection for.

## The Absent Father

While Augusta Gein was large in conviction and angry in spirit, George was quite the opposite. Few people would be imposed or intimidated by Ed Gein's father. By most accounts, George Gein felt like a sigh of a human, a drained man who had been knocked down one too many times and no longer had the strength, nor the will, to get back up again. He was a weak and drunken man and had no involvement in the sons' upbringing. After years of living with Augusta, bringing her two boys, and then slowly fading into a shell of his former self due to his addictions, his own mental health issues, and the suffocating nature of his wife, George was easy to forget and lacked just about every attribute a wife needs in a husband and a son needs in a father. Given her own opinions and personality, it was no surprise that Augusta hated him and thought he was a worthless being unfit to care for their children, let alone hold down a job. She took it upon herself to support the family financially as well as to raise the kids in accordance with her ideals.

George sat by the side and casually watched as his two boys were raised by his wife and taught such twisted and unnurturing things. But he didn't do anything to change her ways. In fact, he didn't even lift a finger to teach his boys another way. Did he agree with her and her religious ways? No, that wasn't it. But for multiple reasons, some within his control and some outside of it, George wasn't going to do anything to put his boys on the right track.

Just wonder how Ed Gein's life could have changed had his father been more present and more caring. George was not the type to toss the baseball around the front yard, teach him how to drive, shave, or manage the world. But what if he was? What if he actually gave a damn and tried to push back against Augusta? Would you be reading about Ed Gein right now? Would the world have experienced the horrors he created?

Of course, we can never know for sure. But what we do know is this: George was not present in young Ed Gein's upbringing. He was hardly there physically and he was completely absent figuratively. That left Augusta to do it all: she would raise her boys, she would educate them, she would teach them what she thought they needed to know. And, in her mind, she would protect them.

In reality, she was scaring Ed Gein in ways that he would never recover from.

Since she couldn't rely on George for absolutely anything, Augusta started a grocery store in La Crosse the year Ed was born, and it made enough money to comfortably maintain the family. She was never a people pleaser and couldn't care less about customer service, but Augusta was able to create a stable, loyal base of clientele that shopped at her store often. While she had started the store as a way for her family to be supported, there was another cause at work, one that shouldn't surprise you given her view of the world.

She put forth a lot of effort and saved money to enable the family to relocate to a more rural region, far from the immorality of the city and the sinners that called it home. While La Crosse was no metropolis, Augusta still desperately needed to whisk her family far away from it. It didn't have enough churches and true believers, she felt. It was lousy with sinners and evildoers, wicked people who wanted to not only corrupt her but her boys and the world around them all. La Crosse was a dark, dark place and the farther away the family could get from it, the better.

From the money that Augusta raised by working the store, the family relocated to Plainfield, Wisconsin in 1914, where they bought a 135-acre farm that was far away from the city and any sinful, inhumane creatures that called themselves human. The farmhouse was far from the city, far from the stores, far from the people. The distance to the nearest neighbors was over a quarter of a mile. That was just the way Augusta wanted it.

You would think that moving so far away from the city would do her good and would make her feel happy and accomplished, like she had followed through on her goal of taking care of her family. But that wasn't so. Even though they were now further away from society, Augusta's fervent opinions only grew more intense. It was if now that she was cut off from the rest of the world she was able to revert to her own, one where the word of God was absolute and towering and truly frightening. And Ed was stuck in the middle of it. His mother had not only cut herself off from the world, she had cut him off too. He was not able to take a walk, he was not able to make friends, he was not able to do anything but stay at home at the farmhouse and sink deeper into his mother's rabid mindset.

Although Augusta worked hard to shield her sons from the outside world, she was unable to completely succeed since the boys had to go to school. In a perfect world, Augusta would have been able to keep her kids at home all year long and educate them solely in the ways of the Bible. But the school system was different back then and homeschooling wasn't as easy as it is now. Additionally, Augusta was working a lot, far too much to be able to give her children the time they needed for schooling. So both of the Gein boys went to the local public school in Plainfield. And despite what sort of person Ed would become later in life, as a child he was actually a decent, if not amazing, student. Ed did well at reading, but his academic performance was only ordinary. He kept up with his grades and seemed to try hard, even when he didn't succeed. But he was far from an out-and-out awful student. He wasn't extraordinary but he also wasn't extraordinarily *bad* either.

And he was actually gaining quite a bit from going to school but it wasn't through learning, but through exploring. Like so many tortured children, Ed found a lot of solace in the world of literature that was presented to him when he started attending school. The stimulation of Ed's imagination and ability to briefly escape into his own universe came from reading adventure novels and periodicals. And it was rewarding for him. Very rewarding. He had been living such a sheltered and truly scary life for so long. His entire existence was predicated and dictated by the worldview of his mother. It wasn't a place that allowed much imagination or creativity, at least not in healthy and happy ways.

But books gave him something new and for the first time in his life, he felt an escape. It was short-lived and it didn't give him the solace he needed, but it did alleviate some of the troubles he felt at home.

Going to public school was one of the first instances that Ed Gein had with the outside world that his mother fiercely hid away from him. And although he wasn't exposed to so much wickedness like he expected, he still got a taste of the world that he didn't like. Ed wasn't a model student and he wasn't a social butterfly. In fact, in many ways, Ed was treated like the odd kid. The weird one. The one that others snickered at and spoke of behind his back.

Because of how he was raised and just due to his overall personality, Ed was different. He didn't seem to be a cruel child (which is odd considering the life he would later live) but he was an easy target for the other kids in Plainfield. He spoke with a slight lisp and was small and meek and had a hard time speaking up and conversing with others. In a number of ways, Ed just felt like bait in a tank full of young, hungry sharks. He was ignored by his classmates because he was timid and effeminate. He didn't have any friends, and when he tried to get any, his mother reprimanded him. She told young Ed that there was no sense in making friends because they were all little wicked, sick monsters full of sin who would only hurt him. No, the only person he really needed to be friendly with was her, she said. And Ed really did feel that he cared for his mother—far more than you would imagine considering the way she treated him and his brother—but he was hoping to connect with kids his own age and make a circle of friends that could give him a new perspective on life. Maybe he would meet other kids who liked to read. Maybe he could find new hobbies to enjoy, new activities to get lost in. Maybe life on the farm wouldn't be that bad if he had some friends.

But it wasn't meant to be. Because of his mother and because of the misfortune of being different, friendship wasn't in the cards for Ed Gein. The young boy was pained by his mother's objection to having friends, but he saw her as the height of virtue and did his best to abide by her strict instructions. Yes, Ed Gein was conflicted about the things his mother said and the way she treated him, but at the end of the day, he really did believe she was right. Mother knew best. Mother always knew best, Gein thought. And she was truly the only virtuous person who could keep him on a path that prevented the fiery and terrible pits of Hell.

You see, when a child is taught these things very young, they are prone to believe them. Take Ed Gein, for example: he had no one else telling him otherwise. What child doesn't believe their parents at a young age? Which kid doesn't think—at least for the formative years of their lives—that their parents are simply looking out for them, would never hurt them, and would never lead them astray? The truth is that all parents impart their own opinions on their children, that's just human nature and it was no different in the case of Ed Gein. The only difference here being that Augusta Gein was convincing her children that the world was a terrible, scary, harmful place. She was also convincing them that unless she was around, there was no one to protect them from all that terror. That's quite a worldview to build in a young child's mind. You can only imagine how it'll grow, fester, and warp over the years as the child gets older.

As Ed and Henry grew older, their mother grew colder. Her attitude was always sour but it got even worse. Perhaps it was the fact that the family was now so secluded and hidden away from the rest of the world. Perhaps it was her anger at her husband. Maybe it was the fact that she saw her boys growing and knew it would be even harder to keep them on a track that she was creating. Whatever the reason, Augusta was becoming even more of a monster as her children came of age. She was seldom proud of her sons and verbally insulted them frequently since she thought they were bound to fail like their father. To be fair, neither child was acting like George Gein but Augusta saw shades of her lazy husband in both of them and repeatedly called them out for being "just like their father." This was a shocking and bewildering accusation for both boys and they found little solace.

## Ed and Henry

Both Ed and Henry had grown close over the years, partly out of necessity. They lived far from any other children and they were in a household that was dangerous and scary. They had to rely on each other for company, for entertainment and for any sort of humanity that was lacking in every other part of their home. Like all brothers, they had a bond that was very close…although it would begin to fray and fall apart in the years ahead.

In the beginning, Ed admired his brother and thought of him as a guy of integrity who worked hard. They became young men together and Ed tried to follow in his brother's footsteps, especially when the family called upon them both to step it up and help. In 1940, George Gein passed away. To Augusta, this was a blessing and she was relieved that her husband was gone. For Ed and Henry, any sort of sorrow they might have had for their absent father had to be hidden because Augusta would not let a single nice word about him be uttered around her. But they were both older now and they could find jobs and help out the family and it was the right thing to do.

So they did just that. Both Ed and Henry took up a variety of odd jobs to help maintain the farm and their mother in the early 1940s as their family adjusted to life without George. Under the leadership and help of Henry, both men were regarded as dependable and trustworthy by the community. Ed regularly watched children for neighbors despite their primary line of work as handymen. As for Henry, he did pretty much any odd job that was laid before him and was also professional, polite, and did his tasks well.

They were both adults now and they were holding down steady jobs but there were already signs that something was different about Ed, something was slightly off.

For example, examine his ease at watching children as a job. While there are many people who love to watch kids, most of them don't do so because they relate to them so much. Most people want to be teachers so they can help young children grow, not so they can be surrounded by people they feel most comfortable with. But Ed was showing signs of stunted growth. His years of being raised by his mother and not having friends in school had created an anti-social and truly troubled young man who lived in a state of arrested development. He had a hard time conversing with others and connecting with people his age. He was much more comfortable acting like a child. This was a warning sign that something was wrong. But it was a warning sign that was missed by many, sadly.

As for his relationship with Augusta, things had progressed in the worst way possible when Ed was a young man.

Over the years, Henry has pushed further and further away from his mom and you can't really blame him. After decades of hearing the same angry rhetoric about heaven and hell and the god and the devil, Henry needed to create space between himself and his mom. He would even push back against her, challenge her, and not let her run the house like an angry minister filled with rage.

But that wasn't the case with Ed, who had only grown closer to Augusta over the years.

To anyone really paying attention, it was clear to see that Ed had an unhealthy relationship with his mom. Henry was, understandably, concerned about it. Henry saw that his brother had issues and he saw that his mother was only making those issues worse. He also knew that Ed was bound for a life of complete reliance on his mother if something wasn't done. Ed believed everything she said and he came back to her again and again like a whipped puppy looking for affection. He really did see evil in the rest of the world and only felt true comfort and peace when he was in the presence of his mom, who would still insult him, demean him, and treat him like trash. Their father was dead and buried at this point, but both Ed and Henry were still compared to him often. Henry's anger with his mom and his insistence on standing up for himself—and sometimes his brother— only grew. In fact, Henry publicly insulted their mother on multiple occasions.

Ed just could not understand why his brother didn't see their mom as a godly, good woman who was simply looking to protect them both. It is clear now that Ed was brainwashed by his mother, raised from a young age to believe such dangerous things, including the fact that he needed his mom in order to survive and be happy and healthy. No one knows for sure if Augusta was aware of what she was doing and how she was influencing her son. She was obviously mentally unwell herself. But by the mid-1940s, Ed's entire life revolved around his mom. Yes, he would work and he would go out with his brother into town but he was stuck to his mom like a magnet.

She could do no wrong. She was always keeping him safe. He was her son and there was no greater role in life.

And anyone who stood in the way of that was simply standing in the way of his entire life.

Ed was humiliated that his sibling did not share Ed's view of his mother as being completely good. He felt betrayed and he felt confused. And there was another emotion brewing inside Ed Gein when he heard his brother speak against their mom, one that he had a hard time regulating or truly understanding.

For the first time in his life, Ed was feeling rage. And it was building inside of him and hard to contain. He was a quiet man, a man who didn't experience this often and had no understanding of what to do when it came racing to the surface. But he was furious with his brother and he wanted Henry's criticism of their mom to stop.

All of this may have contributed to Henry's sudden and puzzling death in the spring of 1944.

## The Death of a Brother

It was just another day at the family farmhouse. Summer was right around the corner and, like all good farm hands, Ed and Henry were rounding up brush and disposing of it.

They were putting out a brush fire on the cool, clear May 16th day that was perilously near to their land. The fire was getting a little wild and it needed to be addressed and kept under control. So the two split up while trying to put it out, according to the authorities. As they went their separate ways and attended to the flames, night swiftly arrived and Ed eventually couldn't find Henry. Ed would later tell authorities that he was greatly worried about Henry and started to panic as his search came up with nothing. Worrying for his lost sibling after the fire was put out, he called the police.

But this is where things get weird and this is when the suspicions arrive. Something was off right from the start after the authorities were called. When the Plainfield police sent out a search team, Ed astonished them all by leading them right to Henry, who was lying dead on the ground. There were various circumstances surrounding Henry's death that worried the officers on duty. For instance, Henry had bruises and was laying on a patch of unburned ground.

How did this all happen? How did Henry, a seasoned pro at tending to brush fires and all things related to the farm, go so far off course? How did he slip or hurt himself—seemingly on nothing—to the point of death? What caused the bruises on his body? And why was his brother Ed, calm and collected, able to locate him right when police arrived even though he said he had been searching for him for hours?

Nowadays, Ed would have looked like a suspect immediately. He might have even been taken in for questioning or perhaps even arrested on the suspicion alone. But not then, not on that day.

In fact, police quickly ruled out foul play despite the peculiar conditions in which Henry was discovered. The simple fact was that nobody could believe that quiet Ed could murder or do something so heinous and cruel, much less his brother. He was seen as a quiet, somewhat slow, and harmless mommy's boy who lived on a farm with his mother and brother. Well, now just his mother. Ed Gein was odd, sure, but he wasn't able to hurt a fly, let alone his very own flesh and blood.

Asphyxiation would eventually be listed as the reason for Henry's death by the county coroner. It wouldn't be until years later that people looked back on the passing of Henry Gein and saw it in a new light. A darker, more sinister—and surely more accurate—light.

Following the death of his brother, it seemed like Ed's life was about to enter a stage that he had been wanting for so long: it was time for Ed to spend the rest of his life with his mom and only his mom. George had passed away, Henry had mysteriously died. Now the farmhouse would be occupied by only two people: Ed and his mom. The rest of Ed's family was gone now but that was more than okay with him because his mother was the only person he needed. They could finally just live together and Ed could rely on his mom for everything without her shouting about his father and without Henry getting in the way with his complicated views.

Yes, it was time for Ed to really get close and connect with his mom and *only* his mom. He would, however, spend a very limited time alone with his mother.

Ed didn't know it but his mother's life was in its final stages. She hadn't been a healthy woman in some time and Ed had tried to ignore that fact, push it away, and pretend like it wasn't happening. But it was impossible to avoid as 1945 rolled around and the years of anger, intensity, paranoia, and general unwellness caught up with Augusta Gein.

After experiencing many strokes, Augusta passed away on December 29, 1945. For months before, Ed had tried to convince himself that his mom would rebound, that she would overcome the strokes and get better and life would be normal again. To Ed, it was almost literally impossible to think that his mother had passed away. It was just something he couldn't comprehend, he couldn't grasp it. How could this woman, who was so strong and so capable and so important to him, die? It wasn't like a woman was dying. To Ed Gein, it was like an entire world was ending. When Augusta died, Ed's foundation and his entire life was shattered in ways that he couldn't wrap his head around or truly grasp.

There was nothing left for Ed. All of his life, his mom was the most important figure in his life. And it wasn't as if Ed just liked being around his mom. No, he was taught from a very young age that she was necessary, mandatory, needed for him to survive. He had built a life where his mother was the central figure, like oxygen he needed to survive. And that upbringing had warped him in so many ways. There was little chance of him changing now, little chance of him living a normal life and not being stuck in the mindset created by his late mother.

And he was so pulled away from the rest of the world, there was no chance that he would know how to reach out for help. The idea of a doctor or a support group or even friends had reeled further and further away from Ed as he got older and spent more time with his mom, pulled away like a reel pulling away from a hungry fish. The chances of his situation changing after his mom's death were not just miniscule, they were so small it was nearly impossible to measure.

After his mother passed away, Ed stayed at the farm and made do with his modest earnings from various jobs. The areas that his mother utilized the most were the upstairs floor, the parlor, and the living room. Ed saw these places as memorials to his mom, a way to keep her and her memory alive. Because of that, he boarded off those areas of the farmhouse. He kept them as a shrine to her and didn't touch them again for many years. He utilized the cooking area and a tiny room off the kitchen, which he used as a bedroom, to live on the lower level of the property.

As for the rest of the house, it began to fall into disarray, starting the journey to the state that it would be in when the police entered so many years later.

It wasn't just the house that started to fall apart. In the years following his mother's death, Ed Gein sank deeper and deeper into a dark pit of dangerous thoughts and impulses. Without his mother to reel him in, Ed was free to do whatever he wanted under the cover of darkness.

In the years after his mom's death, Ed would pass his free time reading adventure books and death-cult magazines throughout his lonely house. He also became oddly interested in the work of Nazi scientists and the morbid and disgusting work they did on the human body during World War II. He followed his pursuits and became obsessed with certain things, puttering around his house and letting his brain wander and dig deeper into the darkest parts of his psyche.

Other times, Ed would lose himself in his odd pastimes, which included going to the cemetery every night.

# A Life Without Mom

Now we enter a phase of Ed's life that was completely and totally his own. When you look at the years before his mother's passing, Ed was living a life that was dictated and decided for him. He didn't make choices, he didn't follow a path he set for himself. No, quite the opposite. Instead, Ed would do as he was told, believed what he was told to believe, and never deviated from what his mom thought was best.

This had a profound and punishing effect on the man's brain and he was now an adult but acted like a child who always needed guidance from his mom. He was not the sort of person who could do much independently. Yes, he was able to hold down a job but people would remark how withdrawn and completely devoid of human interaction Ed was. He didn't seek out friends or people to grow close with. He was never very rude to his clients and he always got his odd job done, but he was never very personable and it was quite clear that he was someone who wasn't used to being one-on-one with people.

Sure enough, that was exactly the case. When he was in the town doing his work such as doing odd jobs or watching a group of local children, Ed would see other people—although he would just pass them by and never stopped to chat. The parents of the children he watched didn't speak much with him, seeing as he was much more at home going one-on-one with the kids instead of the adults. He was very withdrawn and just had no inclination to talk with people his own age.

# Lost in His Mind

Aside from the kids he would watch over, people in the real world felt like a confusing hassle to Ed Gein. But back home, he was able to be completely alone and indulge in his pastimes and hobbies and increasingly dark hobbies. After Ed's mother passed away, he started to feel more and more alone but his desire to try and reach out to others and make connections or friendships withered away and died like a rose on a vine. So instead, he stayed at home and just kept himself busy with the macabre things that kept him fascinated. He read a lot of anatomy books and pulp magazines in his free time. He lived in cluttered, dusty rooms filled with magazines on explorers, Nazis, and natural disasters throughout history.

There came a point when his fascination with these subjects became even darker—and changed from a simple interest to an actual hobby. Through his reading, Ed had learned about the complicated and graphic procedure for reducing heads, exhuming human bodies from tombs, and body anatomy. With his strong reading skills and his abundance of nothing but free time, he developed an obsession. These strange tales filled his brain, and his mind was clouded by disturbing thoughts and facts. To make it even worse, he would try to share these newfound interests with the only people he talked to: children. He was reprimanded for frequently telling some of these disturbing and haunting factoids to the kids he watched. What child should be hearing about the way a human body can be sliced up and preserved? This was a serious warning sign, to put it gently.

But he didn't just read about bodies being cut up and other creepy things. Ed also liked reading the neighborhood papers. In fact, the obituaries happened to be his favorite section.

## Digging in the Dark

It would be the obituaries of the local paper that would open up Ed's mind in new and terrifying ways. For years now, he had these urges buried deep down inside of him. He wanted to do atrocious things and he wanted to explore the human body in ways that were completely shocking. But something kept him in line. Perhaps it was the presence of this dad or brother or maybe it was his mom's domineering ways. But Ed Gein never acted on these desires and feelings—not until his mom was dead and gone and he had the huge farmhouse all to himself, with nothing but space and time to think and think and think about the darkest things in his brain.

If you have ever read the obituaries page, you know that it gives you just a bit of information about the person who died. You get a basic life story and, more importantly to Ed, you find out where the poor soul is going to be buried. This fascinated Ed and it set off an alarm in his mind. All the pieces of the puzzle were there before him and Ed was finally putting together a plan to act out the bizarre and haunting desires he had.

Through the newspapers, Gein learned about the most recent female fatalities in Plainfield and the surrounding area.

This is the moment in Ed Gein's life when everything changed. Any chance of him living a normal life was thrown out the window when he finally acted upon the impulses that he could no longer hold back.

Ed Gein wanted to visit the cemetery, dig up bodies, and then use them for his own desires. Just thinking of him, wandering in the dark through the tombstones, digging into the fresh dirt, and pulling a corpse from the Earth is enough to make your skin crawl. It's hard to fathom how anyone could want to do this, why they would want to do this. But this speaks to the complicated, shattered mind that Ed Gein had.

What did he want with these bodies? It was complicated, to put it gently. There was a sick fascination with the opposite sex that Gein was going to be able to explore through digging up and slicing up and exploring the bodies of the dead. It's no surprise to hear that Ed never liked being among people of the other sex, yet he did have a bizarre fascination with them that he couldn't quite understand or wrap his head around. To him, women were foreign and alien yet…interesting at the same time. There was something about them that made him want to explore their bodies, in more ways than one.

So he would satisfy his needs by going to cemeteries at night. In the following years, after he was caught and all of his plans were unearthed and revealed, Ed Gein would subsequently admit that he had never engaged in sexual activity with any of the deceased ladies he had excavated because "they smelled too bad," but he did like ripping their skin off of their bodies and wearing it. His desire and interest in women was sexual although sexuality definitely came into play with it. You have to remember that for years, he was told that anything related to sex was wrong, sinful, and something to be avoided at all costs. It was a forbidden fruit and, because of that, it was all tied up with the other things that he wasn't supposed to do. While he wasn't having sex with the women he dug up, he was certainly intimate with them in ways that went beyond sexuality.

As for his own identity, Ed Gein was feeling all sorts of things about himself and his gender and who he wanted to be. The closeness he felt with his mom throughout her life and his reliance on her had really shaken up the roles of gender in his life. All of his life, he felt like he was his mother's obedient son and he gladly filled that role. However, with his mother now gone, he craved the sort of motherly presence that she brought. In a way, he wanted to be his mom. Why? So that she would be alive again? So that he could give himself the protection and "care" that she had? It's not entirely clear. But one thing is definitely true: Ed Gein frequently fantasized about being a woman. He was fascinated by their anatomy as well and would read books and look at diagrams and specifically cut into the more private parts of a dead woman's body. Gein would later admit that he was intrigued about what it felt like to have breasts and a vagina.

And his desire to actually be a woman also complicated his views of men and sexuality. Neither straight or gay, Gein started to admire and lust after men in certain ways as he dove deeper and deeper into his quest to become a woman and his nightly visits to the cemetery. Because of the influence and power that women had on males, he was attracted to them. Although it's never been known if he acted on these desires, it is clear that Gein wasn't quite sure who he wanted, who he was attracted to, and even which gender he felt he should be.

After multiple trips to the cemetery at night, Gein amassed a sizable collection of body parts, some of which included skulls that had been preserved. He would later say that he would sink into something of a daze when he would take his shovel and tools to the graveyard. Years and years of desire and wanting came pouring out of him in a semi-psychotic state that he could hardly remember after the fact. It was as if Ed went into an auto-pilot mode, one that allowed him to do what the deepest reaches of his mind wanted without fear of being caught or being reprimanded.

One has to ask: was he actually enjoying the act of digging up bodies and then taking them home, cutting them up, examining them, and living in their skins? It's hard to tell. Of course there must have been some part of him that did get joy and satisfaction from doing all of this. But it's also true that he was acting on instinct. He was simply caving and giving into some of the darkest recesses of his mind. It wasn't exactly pleasure but it wasn't exactly *not* too.

As he spent more and more time doing these horrid things, Ed Gein got more careless and stopped looking after himself and covering his tracks. In fact, there was one occasion when a youngster he occasionally watched over paid a visit to Ed's property. Ed had shown him human skulls that he kept in his bedroom, the boy subsequently said. Ed asserted that the dried-out heads came from the South Seas and were left there by headhunters.

When the little youngster described his encounter to others, his claims were promptly shot down as simply the product of his wild, youthful imagination. Ed Gein did that? the people asked. No way that quiet, sensitive man could be holding a collection of skulls in his home, they remarked. However, the child was then justified when two other young guys went to Ed Gein's property a while later. The preserved heads of women had been seen by them, but they dismissed them as odd Halloween outfits. As you can expect, rumors started to abound in Plainfield about the bizarre things that Ed Gein supposedly kept in his home. He was starting to get a reputation. But how many towns across the country have people that are looked at as "odd" or "spooky" or "weird"? The tales about them are just that: tales, nothing more.

Therefore, the rumors about Ed Gein weren't taken too seriously. But just imagine if they actually were.

Until Bernice Worden vanished a few years later, nobody took those shocking rumors seriously. In fact, Ed would frequently respond with a smile or mention having shrunken heads in his room when others made fun of them. Nobody believed him to be speaking the truth, or perhaps they just didn't want to accept it.

# The Killer Emerges

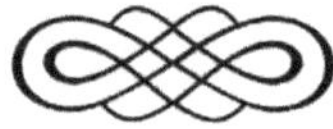

Wisconsin police started to detect an upsurge in missing people cases in the late 1940s and early 1950s. Little did they know that "creepy" Ed Gein was actually putting together a house of horrors that would stain the town and all of Wisconsin for years to come.

Local police were particularly perplexed by four incidents that they couldn't figure out. The first involved Georgia Weckler, a young girl who vanished on May 1, 1947, while traveling home from school. Hundreds of locals and police officers combed a 10 square mile region near Jefferson, Wisconsin in hopes of finding the young girl. Sadly, she was never again seen or heard from. The only concrete leads authorities had were tire prints discovered close to the scene of Georgia's last known whereabouts. There were no plausible candidates. When Ed Gein was finally arrested for his other crimes years later, the Georgia Weckler case was finally reopened after remaining unresolved for so long.

Then six years later in La Crosse, yet another innocent girl vanished from her family without warning. Evelyn Hartley, a fifteen-year-old, was watching a group of children when she vanished. Late in the evening, Evelyn's father called the house looking for his daughter but the phone just rang and rang and rang without an answer.

Hartley's father drove over to where she was babysitting right away out of concern. He knocked loudly but no one came to the door. A pair of his daughter's eyeglasses and one of her shoes were on the floor as he glanced through a window. All the windows and doors of the house were locked when he attempted to enter except for the basement window in the back. He entered the home terrified and saw evidence of a scuffle.

The area was searched, but Evelyn could not be located. A few days later, outside of La Crosse, next to a highway, authorities found some bloodied Evelyn-related clothes. Her family and the community suspected the worst.

Another disappearance struck. Before going out to shoot deer in Plainfield, Wisconsin in November 1952, two men stopped for a drink. They stuck around for a while and enjoyed their drinks and the good company and then they departed for their planned hunt.

The two men and their automobile disappeared without a trace. A thorough search was done, but they were not found. They had just disappeared. Plainfield had stolen away more people in a truly mysterious and haunting fashion.

Mary Hogan, a bartender in Plainfield, unexpectedly vanished from her saloon during the winter of 1954. When they found blood on the bar floor that drip-drip-dripped into the parking lot, the police suspected foul play. Additionally, police found an empty bullet cartridge on the ground. Mary and the other four missing persons had no remains and nothing in the way of relevant evidence, so police could only hypothesize as to what could have happened to them.

But all these years later, you and I can see what the others could not. The only other thing these instances had in common, aside from the mysterious nature of them, was that they were all disappearances that took place around or in Plainfield, Wisconsin. That means they all took place around the farmhouse that Ed Gein remained in, day after day with his increasingly haunting thoughts.

## Investigation

The years passed and no one was around to check on Ed Gein in his nearly abandoned farmhouse. And during that time, it's not entirely clear just exactly what Gein was doing. We know some of the things he would later admit to and some of the things he was suspected of, but the most consequential time in Gein's life is also the most mysterious, and it is now up to experts and analysts to wonder just what he did during this incredibly dark part of his life.

Then when Bernice Worden went missing and was subsequently discovered by the police, everything changed and a lot more light was shed on Gein. However, many more questions were raised too.

Police launched a thorough investigation of the remaining areas of the farm and the surrounding area on November 17, 1957, following the discovery of Bernice Worden's decapitated corpse and other macabre relics in Ed's home. The remains of Evelyn Hartley, Mary Hogan, Victor Travis, and Ray Burgess, as well as Georgia Weckler, were thought to have been murdered and may have been buried on Ed's property. They didn't suspect Gein for those disappearances when they first happened but in retrospect, it absolutely looked like something he would have done.

Held in captivity as the press and local residents went wild at the recent Worden findings, Ed was being questioned by detectives at the Wautoma County Jailhouse. Meanwhile, the serious, important, and dreaded work of the farmstead's excavations got underway.

At first, Gein refused to confess to any of the murders and wouldn't suggest that he even knew about them, let alone had anything to do with them. The cops, however, weren't going to budge and they knew that looking at all those cases and what they now knew about Gein, there was a good chance he was involved in them. They could patiently sit and wait forever, knowing they had time on their side. So they sat and they waited but it didn't take forever. After just more than a day of being silent, Ed started to describe the horrific details of how he killed Mrs. Worden and how he got the body parts that were discovered in his home.

Finally, out of an awful darkness, the horrible details of his deeds were coming to light.

Ed had trouble recalling every detail of each crime. According to him, he had been confused before and during the murder. Remember the "daze-like" state he said that he slipped into? It apparently robbed him of most of his memories during these moments. Still, he told authorities that he remembered hauling Worden's body to his Ford pickup, stealing the cash from her hardware shop, and then transporting both back to his residence. He couldn't recall shooting her in the head with a .22 caliber pistol, which was subsequently determined by an autopsy to be the cause of her demise. He didn't deny that he had done that, he just said he couldn't remember it.

As for everything else found in his home, Ed claimed that he had stolen the additional body parts from nearby cemeteries. Except for Mrs. Worden, Ed adamantly denied murdering any of the dissected individuals who were discovered in his home.

However, after being questioned more for days, he eventually confessed to murdering the local bartender, Mary Hogan. While he knew he did it, he couldn't speak much more about it: Ed once again couldn't remember anything other than shooting her.

## Insanity?

Because of the nature of his crimes and his seeming indifference to it all, Gein's sanity was questioned, and it was proposed that he enter a not guilty plea during the trial on the grounds of insanity. Of course, this had to be more than speculation. Even back in the 1950s, a doctor was needed to prove that a suspect was actually insane and not just twisted.

So the hard work of determining his mental state began. Gein was subjected to a series of intense professional psychological exams. A series of doctors spoke with Gein, asking him very personal things, and examined the results in the most intimate ways. They dug into his mind, which was not a good place to be.

In the end, the results of these tests revealed that he was in fact emotionally damaged. In their interviews with him, psychologists and psychiatrists said that he was schizophrenic and a "sexual psychopath."

In many ways, this diagnosis from the doctors elevated the interest in Gein. Now he was not only a wickedly evil serial killer in the eyes of many, he was also an *insane* wickedly evil serial killer. The press started to learn more about Gein and started to devote a lot of ink and newspaper space to his story and how he came to this point in his life.

The doctors laid it out plainly for authorities—and the press wrote about it. Ed's unhealthy and damaging bond with his mother and upbringing were blamed for his mental state during his killings. The experts said what you definitely suspect already: Gein appeared to struggle with his natural sexual attraction to women, his contradictory thoughts about them, and the abnormal views his mother had ingrained in him. The extreme love-hate sensation he had for women turned into a full-blown insanity over time.

# The Digging Continues

Plainfield investigators, now helped by state and federal authorities, proceeded to examine the area around Ed's property as he was subjected to more questioning and psychiatric evaluations. And what they dug up cast an even darker light on Gein and his home and the secluded and disturbed life he led.

In total, the bones of ten women were found near Ed's farmhouse. Police were dubious, despite Ed's claims, that the eight women's remaining body parts came from nearby cemeteries. They thought there was a good chance that Gein had killed the ladies whose corpses were found. To make sure, the cops had to go into the graves that Ed said he had plundered in order to determine whether the remains originated from female bodies.

Police were ultimately given permission to excavate the graves of the ladies Ed claimed to have desecrated. Every casket had obvious evidence of manipulation, and corpses or portions of the bodies were typically missing.

Another finding on Ed's property would resurface the question of whether Ed had indeed murdered a third victim. Police discovered human skeletal remains on the

Gein property on November 29th. The body was thought to be that of Victor Travis, one of the hunters driving through Plainfield who had vanished. The corpses were promptly analyzed at a criminal lab. Tests revealed that the body was really that of a big, middle-aged woman.

Despite their best efforts, the police were unable to connect Ed to the disappearance of Victor Travis or the three other persons who had gone missing in the Plainfield region years before. They had found many bones and they had many suspicions but, at the end of the day, it was hard to pin more to Gein. But that didn't deny the fact that he was capable of it all. It wasn't hard to imagine Gein doing more than just digging up bodies but actually murdering people.

But, Bernice Worden and Mary Hogan were the only killings for whom Ed could be held accountable. This means that in the grand scheme of things, Gein hasn't murdered nearly as many people as some of the other killers who have captivated America's imagination. But even from the very beginning, it was obvious that people are really drawn to the story of Ed Gein. It was mostly due to how bizarre and creepy the entire saga was. It was unlike anything that American readers and citizens had ever experienced before. And all these years later, people still talk about it, movies are still based on it, and millions are still haunted by it.

68

# Understanding Ed

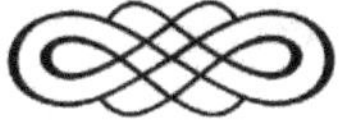

You cannot tell the full story about Ed Gein without talking about how the media and the country around him started to delve deep into the man's story and his motives and his terribly disturbed mind.

Right from the start, journalists from all around the world descended on Plainfield to dig deep into who Ed was and how he turned into the man that could commit such crimes. Ed attained celebrity-like status, and the town gained international—although infamous—recognition. People were horrified by the crimes that were committed on Ed Gein's farm, but they were also drawn to them.

This was a different time for America, a time long before sensational news stories, tabloids, and, obviously, the internet. It was also long before serial killers were really understood.

The age of serial killers would later begin in the 1970s, when Son of Sam, Zodiac, Charles Manson, and others were sadly household names. Ted Bundy and The Night Stalker were just a couple others who became what could be considered sensations.

But before them, America wasn't familiar with what serial killers were and why they worked. The crimes of Ed Gein were quite shocking. Indeed, many people couldn't even stomach the thought of them or couldn't read about them. But they were still so drawn to his story and his wicked nature and the unspeakable things he had done.

He was also of vital interest to the doctors of the world, who wanted to study Gein because he was unlike anyone who had come before him. International psychologists made an effort to understand Ed and what warped him and altered his brain. Everything they determined about Gein found home in the pages of magazines and newspapers and books. Ed rose to fame for all the wrong reasons, as one of the best-known examples of necrophilia, transvestism, and fetishism the world and its medical community had ever known.

Residents in Plainfield had to put up with a barrage of reporters who interfered with their regular activities by asking them numerous questions about Ed. Many of them soon got caught up in the Ed craze and provided what knowledge they had. The world now recognized Plainfield as the residence of the notorious Ed Gein. It was the town that harbored such a haunted and terrifying man. The tales of his personality and his exploits and his parents and his brother and his life were soon all over the world.

Plainfield residents instantly expressed their outrage that Ed would not be held accountable for the killing of Bernice Worden due to his insanity diagnosis. However, the community had few options for influencing the court's ruling. In the end, he wouldn't stay in Plainfield when it was time for him to serve this time. Instead, Ed was admitted to Wisconsin's Central State Hospital in Waupun.

Ed's property and some of his other possessions were put up for sale not long after he was given a mental hospital term. When that happened thousands of people converged on the little town to see what items of Ed's would be put up for sale. His automobile, clothing, and musical instruments were all available to be bought by anyone with the money. All of this created more interest in Gein but it also created some fury among the residents of the small town he came from. The community urged action to be taken because they thought Ed's house was soon turning into a museum and tourist attraction.

The Plainfield Volunteer Fire Department was summoned to Ed's property early on March 20, 1958. The house of Gein was on fire. Witnesses watched in silence and honestly relief as the house swiftly caught fire and burnt to the ground. Because there were no issues with the house's electrical wiring, police assumed that an arsonist was to blame for the fire. Police conducted an extensive investigation, but no culprit was ever located.

Although the majority of Ed's possessions were destroyed by the fire, several items survived. Things such as his automobile and farm machinery were fine and could still be sold at auction—and promptly were. Ed's 1949 Ford automobile, once used to transport corpses from the graveyard to his home, was sold for $716. The man who bought the automobile later displayed it at a county fair, calling it the infamous Gein "ghoul car."

The Plainfield residents believed that the public's interest in Ed would never fade. In many ways, it never did. In other ways, it would mutate, grow, and become normalized. Plainfield would always be known as the quiet cove that grew Ed Gein. And it would attract morbid and curious onlookers for years to come.

But, over the years, other serial killers would come and go and they would capture the attention of Americans. Because of that, the interest in him would subside and become manageable and Plainfield would eventually get back to as close to normal as it could.

As for Ed Gein, the rest of his life would begin in a very different and restricted way.

# Later Life

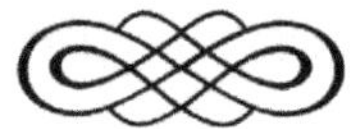

Ed Gein would never hurt another person, but it would be a long time before his ultimate sentence was handed down and he was able to begin serving any sort of set term that was placed on him by a judge.

Following the finding of Bernice Worden, Gein was put in a mental hospital and he would spend years there under careful observation.

Time passed, the world moved on, and Plainfield found some sort of normalcy after all the chaos of the media circus went away. The courts ultimately concluded he was fit to face trial after 10 years in the mental hospital. On January 22, 1968, the trial to establish whether Ed was legally responsible for the murder of Bernice Worden got underway. The trial itself started on November 7, 1968.

Multiple witnesses sat on the stand while Ed silently watched on. The lab technicians who performed the autopsy of Mrs. Worden and a former cop and sheriff were among those who spoke about the crime scene and the man behind it. It didn't take long for Gein's fate to be sealed: Ed was found guilty after just one week due to overwhelming evidence against him.

The first-degree murder charges against Ed were upheld. He was ultimately declared not guilty by reason of insanity and was acquitted because it was determined that he was insane at the time of the murder. But he would never see the free world again. Because of his crime and his mental state, he was sent to the Central State Hospital for the Criminally Insane.

Ed would spend the remainder of his life at the mental hospital, where he had a happy and comfortable existence. He is referred to by his doctors as the ideal patient.

They said that Ed was content in the hospital, maybe more content than he had ever been. He got along quite well with the other patients, but he tended to keep to himself. He kept reading voraciously and always seemed distant, as if his mind still remained in a faraway place. Ed lived a fairly normal life during his time in the mental hospital. He appreciated his frequent conversations with staff psychologists and his treatment team. As well, he thrived at the odd jobs such as rug-making that were assigned to him.

Overall, he was one of the few patients in the hospital who never needed tranquilizers to stay under control. He was completely pleasant, even submissive. It was difficult to tell that he was really insane at all, save from a few anomalies. There were times when he would look at someone with a fixed stare, intense and haunting, as if his faraway feeling was fading and he was starting to think particular things about the person standing in front of him.

And then there were other times, when a female nurse would pass by him and Ed would stop whatever he was doing, lock his eyes onto her, and follow her path as she moved by. It was in those moments that one would remember who Ed Gein was and what he was capable of. He may have seemed gentle and subdued, but there were moments when something inside of him—deep inside of him—came back to the surface briefly.

## The End of Ed

Ed Gein never knew another home after he went to the mental hospital. It was there he would spend the rest of his life. Day in and day out, year after year, he would go to his therapy sessions, meet with his treatment team, and work his small jobs inside the hospital. A few decades passed and Ed grew ill. In the end, he lost his battle with cancer on July 26, 1984. The man that had captured America's imagination for the worst reasons imaginable was gone. The infamous stories of him would live on forever, but the man who was seen as more of a ghoul than a human was gone, now only belonging to the darkest chapters of history books.

His body was sent back to Plainfield where he was sent to one of the cemeteries that he had broken into so many years before. And in a very fitting—and disturbing—final act, Ed Gein was laid to rest next to his mother. For the rest of eternity, Gein will be able to sleep right next to her.

# References

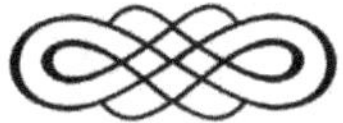


https://www.britannica.com/biography/Ed-Gein

https://allthatsinteresting.com/ed-gein

https://www.history.com/this-day-in-history/real-life-psycho-ed-gein-dies

https://archive.ph/20130121060258/http://www.crimerack.com/2012/04/ed-gein-case-file/

www.ingramcontent.com/pod-product-compliance
Lightning Source LLC
Chambersburg PA
CBHW061706130726
47996CB00006B/2183